FAMOUS PEOPLE

FA[MOUS LIVES]

Biographies of famous people to
support the curriculum.

Queen Victoria

by Harriet Castor

Illustrations by Dave McTaggart

First published in 1997
by Franklin Watts
This edition 2002

Franklin Watts
96 Leonard Street
London EC2A 4XD

Franklin Watts Australia
56 O'Riordan Street
Alexandria, Sydney
NSW 2015

ISBN 0 7496 4359 5 (pbk)

A CIP catalogue record for this book is
available from the British Library

Dewey Decimal Classification
Number: 941.081

10 9 8 7 6 5 4 3 2 1

Series Editor: Sarah Ridley
Designer: Kirstie Billingham
Consultant: Dr. Anne Millard

Printed in Great Britain

Queen Victoria

In 1817 a British princess,
named Charlotte, died. Her
father, the future King George
IV, had no other children to
succeed him. This started a
strange royal race.

George had several brothers.
The race was on between them
to get married and have a child,
because it looked likely that
one day the throne would pass
to them.

In the end, the race was won by
George's third brother, the Duke
of Kent. He married a German
princess and in 1819 she had a
baby girl.

Well
done,
my
dear.

The baby was called Princess Alexandrina Victoria. One day she would be Queen Victoria, but when she was little she was known as Drina.

When Victoria was less than a year old, her father died. Later King George IV died too, and his second brother became King William IV. Now Victoria was next in line to the throne.

Victoria's mother was worried. She thought the King's brothers might plot to have Victoria killed so that they could be next in line to the throne instead.

Victoria was never allowed
to sleep alone, and she couldn't
even go up or down stairs
without someone holding
her hand!

At first Victoria didn't realise she would one day be Queen. When she found out, she burst into tears. But then she said, "I will be good."

Finally, early one morning when Victoria was eighteen, she was told that William IV had died. Queen Victoria's reign had begun.

That night she slept on her own for the first time.

George IV and William IV had not been popular, but the public loved this fresh young queen.

Victoria wanted to work hard at governing the country. She asked her first Prime Minister, Lord Melbourne, for lots of help and advice. Sometimes they spent six hours a day together.

Victoria needed to marry and have children so that everyone would know who would be next on the throne.

Luckily, she fell very much in
love with a prince called Albert.
He was a German cousin of hers.
Because Victoria was Queen *she*
had to propose marriage.
For any ordinary woman this
would have been a shocking
thing to do!

Victoria and Albert were very happy. They had nine children, who all survived (which was unusual in those days). Victoria didn't like babies, though, and she didn't see her children much.

She disapproved of several of her children when they grew up, too – especially her eldest son (later Edward VII). She thought he was going to be a hopeless king.

Albert and Victoria worked together on government work. Albert also set up many new projects.

One of them was the Great Exhibition, celebrating Britain's success in science, trade and industry. It took place in London in 1851 in a huge 'Crystal Palace'. More than six million people came to see it!

19

Victoria wanted Albert to be declared King, but Parliament and the public said no. Victoria's family was mostly German and now she had married a German, too. Many people thought Albert cared more about Germany than Britain.

There was even a rumour that Victoria and Albert had been put in the Tower of London because of this! (It wasn't true.)

21

Victoria hated London. Her favourite homes were Balmoral in Scotland, and Osborne on the Isle of Wight.

The new railways and telegraph communications meant that she and Albert could still keep in touch with the government.

This meant Victoria could go abroad, too, without having to choose someone to rule for her while she was away.

When Albert was only forty-two years old, he died. Victoria was grief-stricken. She was only forty-two herself.

For the rest of her life she kept his rooms just as he had known them – the servants even had to bring clean clothes every morning, and hot water, and scrub out his unused chamber pot!

25

For a long time after Albert's death Victoria hid herself away and refused to appear in public. Her ministers and the people got very fed up with her. One day, as a joke, someone hung a 'To Let' sign on the gates of Buckingham Palace.

Victoria still loved Scotland and spent a lot of time there. She had a favourite Scottish servant, called John Brown. He went with her everywhere, and Victoria allowed him to speak to her much more honestly than anyone else.

She depended on him so much that there were rumours they had got married, and some people nicknamed Victoria 'Mrs Brown'.

29

At this time, the leaders of the two main parties in the House of Commons were William Gladstone and Benjamin Disraeli. Both were Prime Minister several times during Victoria's reign.

Gladstone

Disraeli

Victoria and Gladstone didn't
get on at all. She complained
that he spoke to her as if she
were a public meeting.

Victoria was very fond of Disraeli, though. He charmed and flattered her. She sent him flowers from Windsor and Osborne – usually primroses, which he loved.

Gradually, Disraeli managed to persuade Victoria to go out more often in public. This helped make Victoria popular once again with her subjects.

Britain then controlled lands in many countries, including India. Disraeli arranged for Victoria to be declared Empress of India. This pleased her greatly. Although she never went to India, she kept Indian servants

and ordered a new room to be
built at Osborne for her
collection of Indian furniture
and objects.

She took up daily Hindustani
lessons, too.

There were many new inventions
during Victoria's reign, but
Victoria herself often did not like
change. She didn't like electric
lights, for example, and only
started using them in her houses
and castles long after most other
wealthy people.

When the telephone was first demonstrated to Victoria, she didn't think much of it at all.

She did, though, allow her picture to be taken many times by the new method of photography; and even, towards the end of her reign, took part in a 'cinematographie' – a film.

The way the government worked changed during Victoria's reign, too.

Early on, the Queen took a big role in governing. By the end of her reign, Parliament was more powerful. This was partly because Victoria had hidden herself away for so long. But she was still consulted about what was going on.

In old age, Victoria was an active and very popular queen. After fifty years on the throne she celebrated her Golden Jubilee.

When she'd reigned for sixty years, a new name had to be thought up for the celebration, since there hadn't been one like it before. Someone came up with 'Diamond Jubilee'.

Victoria died in 1901, aged eighty-one. Her children had married into so many other royal families that she had come to be seen as the 'Grandmother of Europe'.

Victoria's eldest son was the great-grandfather of our present Queen, Elizabeth II. And one of Victoria's daughters was the great-grandmother of Elizabeth II's husband, Prince Philip.

Further facts

The Penny Black

The postal system as we know it today was set up in Victoria's reign. In 1839 and 1840 Sir Rowland Hill reorganised the service and started the use of postage stamps. The one-penny stamp, which had a profile of Victoria on it, was known as the Penny Black.

'The workshop of the world'

Between about 1750 and 1850, lots of important developments took place: the steam engine was invented, canals and the first railways were built, roads were improved, new ways of farming were developed and people started working in new places called factories.

These changes came to be known as 'the Industrial Revolution'. Britain became so good at making things and selling them that it was called 'the workshop of the world'.

Children at work

The owners of factories and mines were always looking for ways to save money. One way was to employ children, because they could be paid very low wages. The children often had to work long hours at dangerous work. Later, Parliament passed laws to cut workers' hours and to stop very young children from working at all.

Some important dates in Queen Victoria's lifetime

1819 Princess Alexandrina Victoria is born, daughter of the Duke and Duchess of Kent.

1837 Victoria becomes Queen.

1840 Victoria marries Prince Albert of Saxe-Coburg Gotha.

1851 The Great Exhibition is held in Hyde Park, London. Six million people come to see it.

1861 Prince Albert dies. Victoria is grief-stricken. She wears mourning clothes for the rest of her life.

1876 Victoria is declared Empress of India. Lots of people object but Victoria is pleased.

1897 Victoria's Diamond Jubilee is celebrated.

1901 Victoria dies at the age of eighty-one.